Lasting Love
Building Blocks for a Strong Foundation

Copyright © 2019 Lasting Love Building Blocks for a Strong Foundation

All right reserved. This book or any portion thereof may not be reproduced or used in any manner whatsoever without the express written permission of the publisher except for the use of brief quotations in a book review.

Published by Wisdom Writes Publishing Co. Houston, Texas

ISBN 978-1-733789-7-0-7

Library of Congress Control Number: 2019903294

Cover Design: Evelyn Wilson

Edited by Lovable Impression LLC

The New Living Translation (NLT), copyright 1996, 2004. Used by permission of Tyndale House Publishers, Inc. Wheaton, Illinios 60189. All Rights reserved.

Also used: New International Version (NIV), copyright 1973,1978,1984 by International Bible Society. Used by permission of Zondervan Publishing House. All Rights Reserved. International Bible Society. Used of either trademark requires the permission of International Bible Society.

Also used: King James Version (KJV) which is a public domain.

Limitation of Liability/disclaimer of warranty: While the publisher and authors have used their best efforts in preparing this book, they make no representation or warranties with respect to the accuracy or completeness of the contents of this document and specifically disclaim any implied warranties of any purpose. No warranty may be created or extended by sales representatives, promoters, or written sales materials.

The advice and strategies contained herein may not be suitable for your situations. You should consult with a professional where appropriate. Neither the publisher nor authors shall be liable for any loss, damages, including but not limited to special, incidental consequential, or other damages.

Permissions

Please do take photos of your book for the purpose of reviews or to post on social media, but please do not photograph the entire book. We'd appreciate it if you use the hashtag **#LastingLove** on all posts so that we can create a community of inspiration that is easily found.

DEDICATION

To every married couple that believes in lasting love and building a foundation in God that can withstand the storm. Know that great marriages do not just happen, they are built. Let your journey of lasting love continue forever.

THE MISSION OF LASTING LOVE

To provide a platform for couples to share their testimony, wisdom, advice on relationships, healing, and marriage. To encourage a community of people that marriage and family do matter. To provide an environment of support and encourage marriages to stay together. Also, to provide tools to build a strong foundation to promote healthy family bonds.

ii

CONTENTS

DEDICATION/MISSION i

Contribute by Morgan Jefferson

CHAPTER 1

    After the Vows 1

CHAPTER 2

    Trust 5

CHAPTER 3

    Starting Over 9

Contribute by Anthony Jefferson

CHAPTER 4

    The I Do's, The I Don't, The I Will, The I Won't 13

CHAPTER 5

    Misconception of Love 17

CHAPTER 6

    Unrealistic & Failed Expectations 23

CHAPTER 7

    False Securities 29

CHAPTER 8

    Sexual Ideals 33

CHAPTER 9

    Boundaries 37

CHAPTER 10

    Cold Turkey 41

CHAPTER 11

    Starting Strong Finishing Weak...45

Contribute by Angela Moore

CHAPTER 12

    How My Wounds Affected Me..51

CHAPTER 13

    Healing Pass Your Hurt 55

CHAPTER 14

    My Healed Place 59

Contribute by Pastor Edna Sias

CHAPTER 15

    A Wise Woman Builds Her Marriage..................................63

Contribute by Apostle Darrell Sias

CHAPTER 16

    The Binding Together of Ish and Isha (Man & Woman)......67

Contribute by Jamal and Kim Diamond

CHAPTER 17

    Purposed To Be Together 71

Contribute by Jasmine Addison

CHAPTER 18

    Rebuilding From The Ground Up..75

CHAPTER 19

    Being Anchored on A Solid Foundation................................85

Contribute by Bryant Addison

CHAPTER 20

    The Jagged Emotions of a Man 91

CHAPTER 1

After the Vows

Matthew 19:4-5

And he answered and said unto them, Have ye not read, that he which made them at the beginning made them male and female,

And said, for this cause shall a man leave father and mother, and shall cleave to his wife: and they twain shall be one flesh?

I remember the day we said, "I do" at the altar that day went by so fast. I remember getting my hair and makeup done earlier that day and running behind rushing to the church. It all went by so fast; the vows at the altar. The lighting of the unity candle, the sand covenant, the kiss, and the jumping of the broom. We took a lot of pictures, enjoyed our cake, talked to family and friends then off to the honeymoon. In one day, we have now made the decision to no longer be two, but now start the journey of becoming one. We can say that the process is easier said than done. If you are willing to put in the work, you can have lasting love in your marriage. Will it always be perfect? No. Will you have ups and downs? Yes, but through it all you will know that your spouse will be the one person that is committed to always being your support for a lifetime! So, make up in your mind now that the foundation that is being built in your marriage will be one that will stand throughout time.

Over the years my husband and I have witnessed marriage ceremonies that have cost $20,000 and up and did not last a year. We are sharing that information to say that the amount of money spent on a wedding does not prove how committed you are. This should encourage you not to merely focus on physically wedding, but on the spiritual union of becoming one.

Society promotes the glamourous side of marriage as the prettiest: the wedding dress, the biggest ring, the tallest cake, the biggest wedding party, the longest train, to the most elegant decor, and fireworks. We must remember that the most important part is the covenant of two people. Many couples will prepare for the picture-perfect wedding without thinking twice about how we can ensure that the love will last. This is not a question you can answer quickly, but with the insight and guidance of Holy Spirit you can began to build a firm foundation.

Now the courtship has ended, and you have moved from a committed relationship to a covenant relationship under God. So now we move from just thinking about what we are going to do today to planning and making decisions for the future together. Not every marriage will be the same, but similar in some areas. You must first seek God and ask for the wisdom on how to build your marriage from the foundation up. Now we have the united the two becoming one. This means you now see all of each other.

Genesis 2:25 And they were both naked, the man and his wife, and were not ashamed.

Some of the things you would never reveal are now out in open. You now have a wife, you now have a husband, and you will begin to see each other in a totally different light. This union is an example of Christ and the church. We reveal our strengths and weakness to the Lord, knowing that Christ will still love us the same. This same relationship now exists between a husband and wife. You can experience a oneness that is one of a kind. Marriage was God's plan from the very beginning to have a union that would be blessed.

Genesis 1:28 And God blessed them, and God said unto them, be fruitful, and multiply, and replenish the earth, and subdue it: and have dominion over the fish of the sea, and over the fowl of the air, and Over every living thing that moveth upon the earth.

CHAPTER 2

Trust

Proverbs 31:10-12

Who can find a virtuous woman? For her price is far above rubies. The heart of her husband doth safely trust in her, so that he shall have no need of spoil. She will do him good and not evil all the days of her life.

I remember the day my husband and I had the biggest fight ever. The marriage license came off the wall. Words of disappointment came forth and the pain I saw in my husband's eyes were unbelievable. My heart was beating extremely fast my thoughts were racing not sure of what to do. A pillar of trust had come crumbling down due to miss handling information. Why did I make this mistake? How could we ever recover from this avalanche of occurrences in our marriage. It took a lot of prayer, and rebuilding to reestablish trust again in our home without any more second guessing. I learned that even when you think your putting sensitive, confidential information in the ears of others, they will not safeguard it like your spouse. Some information is meant for you, God and your spouse only. Have you ever heard the saying that every best friend has a best friend? In so many words your personal information may end up in the ears of someone else's best friend and so on. All matters first need to be discussed with the Holy Spirit for guidance on how a matter should be disclosed, shared, or from whom to receive counsel from for certain marriage matters.

Proverbs 31:11-12 The heart of her husband with safely trust in her, so that he shall have no need of spoil. She will do him good and not evil all the days of her life.

Building pillars of trust in your marriage matters. Without trust you're not able to have the support t to hold up the covering of your marriage the roof. The roof is the part of the home that keeps out the elements. The roof protects the home from the sun, wind, and rain. Make the decision to build the pillars of trust in your marriage and family. Be the wife where the husband's heart can be safe and give him no reason not to trust in you with all that he has.

CHAPTER 3

Starting Over

Isaiah 44:18-19

Remember ye not the former things, neither consider the things of old. Behold, I will do a new thing; now it shall spring forth; shall ye not know it? I will even make a way in the wilderness, and rivers in the desert.

It is ok to reinvent your marriage or start over! Watching HGTV I said to my husband it is crazy how a contractor and a designer can tear down a house to the bones and rebuild a house and it looks totally different. He replies, "as long as the foundation is good you can rebuild." This is true when it comes to building a marriage your foundation must be built on God. So, when the trials and temptations come you have a foundation that will stand. No matter how fiery the disaster may be with God you can rebuild. For example, if you think about a volcano when it erupts you do not want to be anywhere nearby the hot lava or dangerous gases. We also know that once the lava decomposes it causes the soil to become fertile, which provides nutrients and minerals that are beneficial to plants. Also, many beautiful islands are formed from volcano eruptions. So, when the heat comes, how you handle it matters. Have your grandparents ever told you do not go to sleep angry? It is wisdom in that old saying.

Ephesians 4:26 says

"Be ye angry, and sin not: let not the sun go down upon your wrath."

How many times have you gone to sleep angry and upset without having a conversation with your spouse about what's on your mind or heart? Now that you gone to sleep angry you've have a bad dream or a restless night, and nothing was resolved. We have more than once, and we know it just doesn't end well. We have also had moments when we have said unbelievable things about each other and our marriage and have had to repent to each other and God for the behavior we allowed to happen while being angry. Anger is an open door for the enemy to jump in and wreak havoc on your marriage. So, we had to learn the art of communication with each other in times of anger or disagreements with the coaching of the Holy Spirit mending us back together after the argument. A lot times the Holy Spirit would begin to convict both of us at the same time, convicting us to apologize to one another regarding where we both have erred. Do not allow anger and pride to get in the way of having a lasting love.

CHAPTER 4

The I Do's, The I don't,
The I Will, The I Won't

Ecclesiastes 9:9

Live joyfully with your wife whom you love all the days of the life of your vanity which God has given you under the sun, all the days of your vanity: for that is your portion in this life, and in your labor which you perform under the sun.

Marriages fail today not because you didn't try, but because neither person knew what to do during trouble. We would like to think that we have it all together, and we know it all, but the truth is we don't. Many of us began our courtships with the wrong mindset and ideals, then try to build a relationship leading to a faulty foundation. Many of us learned about how to manage and interact in relationships through the wrong sources. Those error ideals became our behavior, then ultimately that behavior became the very personality that we brought into the relationship as baggage. Nobody goes into any relationship expecting it to fail, but at times we don't know if it's built to last either. So, what are we supposed to do? Who do we turn to? The radio and listen to love songs, TV hoping to come across a talk show featuring your unanswered questions or unresolved issues? We seek many avenues for relationship advice, but we neglect the first source we all have access to. Where did relationships begin and where did they start? It all began with our Father in the kingdom of heaven. Some may say in the garden of Eden. Either way God designed the formula to build and sustain courtship between man and woman.

You may have journeyed on a roller coaster of ups and downs, joyous times, or situations where you truly believed the best solution is to just walk out. Over time, through trial and error I myself have learned that walking out is not the best solution for solving any problem. In fact, it only makes it worse. Love is the greatest defense, we have in conquering any attack that edges our way. I have reached a point in my understanding that I know when people are going through relationship problems with what they post on social media. Many times, people go to social media not only to vent, but to look for an amen corner full of like-minded individuals to bat the flame and pacify your anger. This is how you end up turning in the wrong direction using the wrong advice for you and your house. One of the biggest misguided views I see that individuals debate over or agree on is their ideas of roles in the relationship; whether it be sex, intimacy, what you would or wouldn't do or put up with. Being that we live in a fast pace and influential age where information and support are right at our fingertips the second we want it, we come across so many opinions and information that may or may not fit into your marriage. We must be able to hear through the spirit to discern if such information is reliable and relates to our situation. What we need to realize is, no two people are the same when it comes to marriage. You are trying to join two backgrounds, ideologies, teachings, and points of views as one. The truth is many of us learned how to operate and cope in relationships with those around us from parents, grandparents, friends, or the TV. When we listen, does it alter how you act in your relationship? Does it change the dynamic of your relationship? People do change, and I sincerely hope for the better, but then some may change for the worst. Not because we want to but because we don't know any better.

CHAPTER 5

Misconception of Love

Many of us have learned about relationships through others or our own past experiences many misconceptions have been created in the way we think and what we believe love is. Those who are married and those who desire to be married at some point in time heard friends or family share their journey and insight of what a marriage should be. However, do they even know and understand what marriage is or what it takes to keep a marriage? We should always take this insight with a grain of salt. Did you know that with as many people living in the world today it is said that there are no two fingerprints alike? So why do we try to cookie cutter our marriages as if it is a one size fits all. Many outside statistics say that most marriages end in divorce before the five-year anniversary. Why is this? Why do marriages fail to begin with? Why is the divorce rate steadily increasing? You don't need worldly statistics to tell you this just look at those around you. Much is due to the misconceptions of love we have created for ourselves. It all starts with looking for love and companionship in the wrong places. Put that together with the wrong ideas of what love is, and what it looks like just screams disaster. This misconception arises because people go into marriages treating it like a buffet of choices that you can mix and match at your choosing. Cherry picking the best parts of marriage while skipping over the less desirable parts. God forbid the buffet line runs out of your favorite dish, now you are ready to leave, or you become unsatisfied with what you have. You must get to a point in your understanding to see that nothing being built to last can be built overnight. As I mentioned earlier, this microwave ready-made society, we live in has affected our patience and we jump in head first prematurely before we listen to what God has to say. We want it right now, we want it perfect, and we want it exactly how we see it in our minds. It's like clicking google search, type in what you want and what you are looking for and there you have it. So now you believe that you have just what you asked for, so why did it not turn out exactly how you pictured it? I can tell you why, somewhere between wanting what you want and not understanding that God knows what you need, your misconception took over then you fall in love with a fantasy. Rather than embracing the reality that you cannot build the perfect relationship understand that through God you can build a perfect love in turn forming the perfect bond in your marriage. Yes, I said it having a perfect love is very real and very possible. I was blessed with my soul mate, but many do not experience this in their lifetime because these misconceptions hold us back from what we really need for what we think we want. Ask yourself when you began to Lego build your spouse and dictate how you want your marriage did you ever stop to ask God if this is what you need. The reality is we would like to share our relationships with the world, but being married and sharing your union with the world should not be hinged on these misconceptions. Love is not an adolescent relationship goal to wear matching outfits with matching shoes. Relationship goals are being on the same wavelength mentally and spiritually. Having the same desire to build wealth, living in good health together, and building the life two of you could imagined. Relationship goals should build an unbreakable bond with a love that can stand beyond the uncomfortable struggles. This is the difference between a true lasting love and love built on misconstrued ideas. To experience this type of love, you must change your mindset of what you thought love was then seek God for the answer of what love is. The reason why more people do not experience this is the willingness to put forth the effort it takes with the time, the discipline required to achieve such wisdom. This is where we need to spiritually evaluate the insight and advice we receive. To see if it lines up with what God told us in the beginning what your marriage would be. Social media, single friends who cannot keep a relationship, daytime talk shows, music, nor movies are the best way to go about building your marriage or trying to understand your spouse. Leading magazines can't help you, well known talk show host can't mentor you, and a Mad Black, or Think like a movie is not going to fix it. So, we can't look for answers anywhere else other than the Kingdom of God.

God created love and gave woman to man for companionship. Therefore, Kingdom minded people should be raised up and set in the place of intercessory to present a Godly example. This is a prayer that my wife and I pray; it is that our marriage will be a beacon light for other married couples and those desiring to be married. Many have failed to do this, and it has led hundreds of thousands to create mis implications and misconceptions of love and what love looks like in marriage. In turn, this has led to divorce, broken marriages, hardened hearts, guilt and even regret. How do we rid ourselves of these misconceptions of love? First, we must check our source of information and see if it is in line with what God has said in our own personal life. I know we love our friends and family, but they are not always a reliable source for our marriages. Remember, they are our friends and family so when problems arise letting them in can cause a bias point of view. More than likely they will support you even if you are wrong. They may see you as the victim when you could be the wolf squeezing in sheep's clothing. Next, question your intentions because many of us get into marriages for the wrong reasons to begin with, whether it be to spiritually legalize sex before God (even though He knows our hearts), to have someone by our side, to flaunt in front of our friends,(that may not have what we have), or because you become envious while seeing others jumping the broom, so you want to do it too. This is what I call the "Me too marriage", which don't last very long. Loving someone and sharing your life with that person in a marriage is wonderful. However, let's dispel the misconceptions of love by finally renewing our minds of what love is. The Bible outlines in 1 Corinthians 13: 4-8 of what love is and what it is not. To bring it closer to home love is not sleeping in separate beds at night, living in separate houses, living separate lives from one another, competing with material possessions, or downing and complaining about one another behind each other's back when we are angry or frustrated. Love is being able to talk it through reaching a common ground, bringing disagreements to an end. Understanding biblical roles for the husband and wife in the home and marriage, building trust not allowing each other to become jealous or insecure.

Sharing intimacy outside of sexual actions and loving one another not only through the good times, but also through the bad. It is very possible to continue to fall further in love and remain as one while going through a storm as it is in the sunshine. This is what love should continually be, loving until there is nothing left to build and then loving even the more.

CHAPTER 6

Unrealistic & Failed Expectations

Looking for the wrong examples of marriage or looking at someone else's marriage and expecting yours to look, sound, and be just like those you are watching can become a very real danger to the health and stability of your own marriage. Remember, no two marriages are the same. I know you may want a marriage like mom and dad, grandma and grandpa or even those you see in leadership roles. However, the truth is you don't know what they went through throughout the course of their marriage behind closed doors, or how they were able to make it to the point they are now. We only see the beginning, middle, or the result of other's marriages looking from the outside which is not always the best place to judge whether you want the same thing for your marriage. Now I am not saying you cannot look at a couple loving one another and desire the same, but I am saying you must know the entire story first. If you talk to married couples, they will tell you there is always a story between the beginning, middle, and end results. I myself grew up around long-lasting marriages averaging 20 to 40 plus years and no it wasn't a smooth road for either person.

The average couple or individual may not understand that this type of union takes works along with dedication. It takes a level of love that does not compare to a mere two-year courtship filled with puppy love, infatuation, and lust. Those unrealistic expectations creep in at the beginning when we are on our best behavior trying to impress one another. This is when we believe we are on our way to becoming the guru of love. We flirt with one another, text sweet wooing messages throughout the day, when you see each other you can't take your attention away from the other. So, what happened between then and now. I remember my mother telling me before I got married that I should not start anything that I do not intend to continue doing. I did not totally grasp this until I met my wife. See when you are just dating there are certain things that you do under certain self-obligated intentions not in the pursuit of love. You are trying to sweep the other off their feet, but they soon learn once you have lifted them off their feet you quickly let them fall flat. This is not just things like showing up with flowers, opening doors, cooking dinner, holding hands, long conversations, even doing things you are not comfortable with, but you do them anyway. All because your desired result is slightly different when you are dating verses when you are married. What you see someone else do in their relationship or what you think should be done to get the attention you want to receive may work during the infant stages of relationships. But doing this we set standards and build expectations, we do not intend to keep. Ultimately, changing the dynamic of your relationship. I am not saying you should not do these things for one another, but I am saying have the right intentions when doing them. Do it out of genuine love with a desire to continue to perform such courtesies. These are the simple nuances that can make a difference in someone.

However, these are not the expectations I am talking about. I am referring to expectations that we put on each other due to our own beliefs or motivations. We get so engulfed with what we expect from others that we do not see the heavy pressures being placed on ourselves and our spouses. Sometimes we do not even know that we are putting this kind of pressure on our spouse because they are so busy trying to be everything you are asking them to be that they fail to be who God intended them to be. When you do not know what you need, you become unsatisfied with what you have ending up placing more on each other than is necessarily possible. We want our spouse to be super husband, and super wife, to super mom and super dad. The handyman, the maid, the perfect lover in bed, the bread winner, and the problem solver all while expecting were at your beckon call whenever you need. Setting the bar so high with expectations that if they fall short and cannot meet those needs it becomes a deal breaker.

Overly zealous expectations in your marriage can cause unintended problems with unforeseen consequences. We like to forget our shortcomings while expecting the other to carry the weight of what we can't bear ourselves. Remember, you cannot ask anything of anyone you first are not willing to do yourself. This can also coincide with what we are allowing into our ear gate and eye gate. We can look at something and begin to envy and lust after what has caught our eye or sounds flattering to our ears without knowing it. We shouldn't watch what some else is doing in their marriage and simply assume that our spouse should be doing just that. Your wife may not be an amazing cook and your husband may not be a mechanically inclined handy man so we should not put this type of pressure on one another. When you do and those needs are not met, you can begin to feel as if you have been short changed leading to problems in your home. Learn and understand the strengths and qualities in your spouse appreciate and begin to cultivate right there. What we may think is or is not beneficial to you personally may or may not be what your marriage needs. So do not criticize or see any less of one another while trying to compare them to someone else. Many times, we do just that setting up mental flow charts and spreadsheets listing the pros and cons comparing our spouses to exes, other spouses or even what you have seen or heard on tv. This mistake is guaranteed to lead to failed unrealistic expectations. Love is not something that is bared only on our own wishes and perceptions. It is a collaboration of honoring one another, appreciation, care, and the willingness to take the good and wonderful attributes of the other while transforming their weakness into their greatest strength. This is not about lowering your expectations this is about setting Godly expectations and goals that both you and your spouse know, understand, respect, and you both are willing to work to meet. If by God's own admission, married you to someone that is not who you believe they are supposed to be. Basing this on your perceptions, then you have failed to see that person for who they are. You then try to turn them into who you want them to be. This is not fair to ask of anyone. If you know their potential and you know they can be more than who they are currently there are ways to encourage those things to come to past. Such as prayer, communication, patience, and an open understanding where you both desire to be.

You may think that God has given you a work in progress, but the reality is he gave you just what both of you needed for where you are on your journey. Your expectations must be spiritually realistic to who that person is and where God is taking you both. To receive and expect the best out of each other, continuing to grow in lasting love, you must keep this in mind. Remember marriage is not a personal hobby you pick up and work on for a certain duration just to past the time. Marriage is not a fad that goes out of style, nor is it something you try out because the people around you are doing it and it looks good from the outside looking in. It is not something you engage in just to say I have a husband or wife, but soon as real-life hits you are ready to leave. Marriage is not a coat you drop off at the thrift store just because it no longer fits or get you the attention you were once looking for in the beginning.

CHAPTER 7

False Securities

We often find ourselves desperately searching for someone to love and being loved causes us to attach ourselves to the slightest emotional feeling and regarding it as love. Due to this we start putting our hope into something or someone that is not in our best interest; emotionally, mentally, or spiritually. You come to believe that having a ring on your finger along with just anyone on your side to call your own is all you need to feel loved. This is how you end up short changing yourself and being deprived of true agape love. You have allowed flattering words, a warm body, and a shiny piece of jewelry to influence what you now regard as being loved. Those things are only seen on the surface leading you to confuse your self-vindication. Neither can gauge how much you are loved. Believing in those things as the bond of love that will hold your marriage together gives you a false sense of becoming one. False securities cause us to be content with what we are given no matter how it is wrapped or presented. This erred viewpoint can cause one to think there is something wrong with who they are when these false senses of reality are not the tie that will keep your marriage together.

When we come into a union harboring such misconceptions, we begin to operate from a place of false hope, believing in love not by its actions but by what it appears to feel like. When you settle for what love looks like rather than what love is, you misinterpret what the relationship truly is. The weight of carats of the diamond, the shine of the band on your ring, nor the extravagance of your wedding can truly show you the depth and breadth of love or the strength of the union. When did these things become the standard for how much you love and want to be with someone? God is not interested in the cost of your wedding or the size of your wedding party. Those are our concerns that mean nothing to the marriage. When all the guests are gone is when the journey starts trying to come together as one. Many people get so caught up in the excitement of finding someone and not being lonely they miss out on the most important part of the union, upholding the covenant and the sanctity of the marriage. Such a covenant under God should not be taken lightly, and the person God has given you in marriage should not be taken for granted. Sadly, multitudes of married couples have said that they feel lonely while in the same house or room with their significant other.

Why is this? Is it because the newness of the marriage has worn off? Is it due to placing your hope in an artificial view of love? I have witnessed firsthand the consequences of artificial love. Being invited to wedding ceremonies where so much time and effort went into the wedding only for the union to abruptly end months into the marriage. Do not find hope in the superficial but place all your hope and faith in God. He is the one who empowers your bond and holds your union together in lasting love. You must build on more than just how beautiful your wedding was or the honeymoon experience. This is not what being married is about. This way of thinking causes marriages to fail because your false securities have built an unstable foundation. You cannot build a home on unstable ground because soon as the rain come, and the winds blow your home will surely be moved and possibly crumble. Your mindset must be in tune with each other. You must be attracted to more than what's on the surface. If your marriage is based on surface vanity, and a vague sense of love there can be no depth. Your marriage needs a real Godly substance. This is what nourishes your bond. How do you move away from the superficial into sustenance? You must know what God has planned for you according to his will over your life. Then you must establish a Godly connection with whom you desire to marry. This is obtained only through spiritual understanding. Marriage is not a competition, competing against other couples for the sexy wife, the most handsome husband, the biggest and brightest ring, or the most expensive wedding. It is about coming together as one in the sight of the heavenly Father and building a lasting union. There is nothing wrong with having these things, but they are not enough to keep you nor sustain your marriage.

CHAPTER 8

Sexual Ideals

A topic we are very familiar with is the concept of sex. There is a common mistake that so many make, that is putting sex before the marriage. People have said if the sex is not good, then it is a deal breaker. Some even bring perverted experimentation in the bedroom inviting people into your marital bed which is to be sacred between husband and wife. Where did these ideas come from? Does how good the sex carries as much importance to the marriage as love, honor, and support. The truth, whether you will admit it or not many of us learned about sex through perversion. The provocative late-night movies, the magazines hidden in the closet, and pornography. Some may have learned by listening to older siblings, family members, or friends telling you about their promiscuity. These seeds being planted take root and grow and whatever seed you plant that's what will grow. After you have reached the age of maturity where you want to experiment you feel there is a green light to do as you please. But did you know this has only tainted your ideas of what sex in marriage should be. You want your husband and wife to perform what you have seen in pornography, but this is not love making this is the acting out of lust and perversion. What you have allowed into your eye gate has placed in you a skewed idea of what sex is and what is its intended purpose.

Sex has turned into a hot bed of self-pleasure not only through masturbation but also sexual indecency. The sexual imagery you grew up watching and may still watch as an adult opened you to perverse intimacy. You start to believe that this is what sex is. I must tell you that you would be wrong. We must be careful of what we allow in our home and invite into our bedroom. Such deviant things open opportunities for the enemy to get into your mind and eventually overtake your actions. This fills our consciousness with a narrow understanding so you start feeling that you are unsatisfied. It is not that you are unsatisfied, but the monster you have created wants more. The spirit of perversion knows no boundaries when in the pursuit of pleasure. This spirit has led many to adultery, lust, masturbation, and a total misunderstanding how to engage in sexual intimacy with our spouse. This is something that I had to learn and experience for myself to better understand how this can get in the way of having a passion filled sex life in your marriage. Misguided ideas about sex can tear down your relationship when you are only after self-gratified pleasure. You start to put more on your spouse than what they are comfortably willing to do making them feel inadequate. When it is only you that has developed an unhealthy misunderstanding of sex. Sexual intimacy is a big part of being married, but what if I told you that God is the way to create a beautiful intimate satisfying sex life. God created it and he created you therefore, he can teach you how to satisfy one another. It may sound strange to hear that inviting God into the bedroom can improve your sex life. But he can not only improve it, he can sustain it. I remember getting counseled before and after getting married to my wife and we were told that my wife is to be my fantasy and my ecstasy. Also, God can teach us how to have good sex. It was a little weird hearing this at first until I received spiritual revelation what was being said. The first thing is we must empty what we learned throughout the years of perversion and fornication to connect not only physically but mentally, and spiritually with our spouse. If God is the bond holding you together, why would he not know what you need to satisfy each other. The wrong images on TV and movies has clouded our view of sex. The bedroom is not to be defiled and every time we bring in with us thoughts and ideas of what we have seen and experienced that is inducing a mental form of infidelity. Really think about it for a second where exactly did all the different versions and actions of sex come from. We know that much of what has made its way into the bedroom did not come from the kingdom of heaven but from the pits of hell. Was that a bit harsh, yes, but the truth must come forth regardless of how it makes us feel. Sex is one of the most intimate forms of bonding married couples can share. If we don't understand its significance, we can fail to unlock a level of pleasure that can only be reached once we connect on a high level mentally and spiritually.

CHAPTER 9

Boundaries

In order to further grasp what it takes to please each other without demanding or expecting more than what either of you are comfortable with, you must set boundaries. This is one mistake that people make in the beginning fail to do. Boundaries are not there only to gauge how far you are willing to go, but they are there as a reminder that you have set borders that the two of you will not cross. This is due to so many having a perverted, misconstrued idea of sex and certain things you now believe must be done to make the sex better. Which many of these things God never intended to be part of lovemaking. Some of the things we have tried before may not be part of your spouse's personality, but you force such uncomfortable situations without knowing the damage you could be causing. You may have tried some things in the beginning to get and keep your spouse, but now you feel that you do not have to do those things anymore once you become married. Therefore, boundaries need to be set in the beginning and not when it is convenient for you (after you have received the ring). This is where many problems with adultery and infidelity starts. People have said that what your spouse won't do someone else will. This does not justify breaking your covenant between each other and God. Such boundaries are needful; not just for sex but for other aspects of marriage as well.

Such as finances, spirituality, family and friends getting in the middle of your marriage, children, and even with disagreements. It is especially a must that boundaries are set concerning household obligations all the way down to respect. What you allow from the start can potentially carry over into your marriage. Before you get to the alter you say and do certain things you believe will keep your partner happy as well as content. Finally, you stand at the altar, say I will, and I do giving your new spouse the reassurance that those things will continue into the marriage. However, once you leave the alter, not a day after the honeymoon you cease and desist. Your spouse will be expecting the same from you as before. Suddenly those things you once did or said you would do in the beginning turns it into I don't, and I won't.

This is a form of false advertisement and can lead to problems in both your home and bedroom. You cause someone to believe they have found the one with all the perfect qualities only to find out they were pulled into an illusion. This not only leaves you with failed expectations, but you now want to set boundaries only after the commitment has been sealed before God.

Boundaries are not there to enforce your way of thinking on the other, they are there to give notice and understanding that certain things will not be allowed in the marriage. There is more to marriage than just sex and sex acts so we cannot get the wrong idea of it and began to perform all types of acts we think will keep each other happy. That kind of intimacy carries only a temporary feeling, but lasting love is performed through action and deeds. Just as the Father expresses his love towards us, we can do the same with our spouse. Talk to each other, teach and learn what pleases the both of you not only in a physical manner but also mentally. There are more areas of the body to stimulate other than sexual organs.

CHAPTER 10

Cold Turkey

Our sexual Ideas must be reconfigured, and boundaries must be set so that we understand that sex and intimacy is not something that can be given or rationed out at your choosing. These areas are not bargaining chips that you use to get what you want. They are not set to treating one another for only reserved special occasions such as birthdays and anniversaries. This is not something meant to be held hostage because you felt some type of way at the time. Making your spouse suffer until you are through feeling emotionally can cause your marriage to suffer. This can also open doors to let in issues such as resentment, entitlement, and more anger. But, how? You thought you were doing the right thing by holding out, but it backfired. By no means is sex a makeup tool that sets everything back on the right track nor is it an apology. This is something I have learned through experience. When having issues in my marriage, I believed by not letting my wife touch me I was somehow getting back at her because I was angry. I wanted her to feel what I was feeling. We both did this to each other, and it presented more problems that could have been avoided. This was the wrong way to go about things because in the end, I was the only one still upset. I can admit we do not stay mad at each other long no matter if I am ready to get over it or not. All she has to do is smile at me, it is a double-bladed sword and I believe she knows this. On one hand it can end bickering quickly, but on the other hand (I think) she just wants me to change the subject. We had to teach one another to see what buttons are not to be pushed, and what are the overload levels before we lash out at one another.

Sex and communication were two things that we thought we could use to get back at each other. Whenever she would hold out, I quoted 1 Corinthians 7:4-5 as if to say she is going against God's word. I did not want to go up to verse 3 because I wanted to make my point. There were times when I did not understand that she may be tired, and I would again quote Proverbs 5:17-19 trying to give myself permission to force myself on her not knowing that was only pushing her further away. In this error I began to allow thoughts to seep in of her committing adultery because surely this is the reason why she is not interested in making love to me. I was foolish and we were foolish together. We allowed sex to turn into an issue of its own. I began to treat her the same way, no love, hugs, kisses, or intimacy of any kind until she gave me what I wanted and when I wanted it, (cold turkey). In this mindset God rebuked me, he reminded me of Psalms 5:17-19 and 1Corinthians 7:4-5 that I tried to use against her. He scornfully told me that I have a commandment to love my wife and treat her as he has commanded us to do as husbands. I can admit this was a wake up call for me. I no longer withheld intimacy from my wife out of spite I had to repent, and it was after this I apologized to my wife as she also did to me. We are wiser and more mindful now understanding that sex and intimacy is bigger than the both of us. What if God withheld his love from us until we did what he wanted us to do? This is a place that I can't imagine being in. You must keep sex and intimacy in a loving place between the two of you. If you want to go cold turkey this is better suited for those who are not married to abstain from fornication. Not being intimate with your spouse out of selfishness, spite, and bad intentions can leave doors open for things to get in such as lust, masturbation, and flirting with other people. The enemy plays with our minds and perception. We allow this to happen when our minds and marriages are not guarded with prayer and the right intentions.

CHAPTER 11

Starting Strong Finishing Weak

Proverbs 5: 18-19

Let your fountain be blessed, and rejoice with the wife of your youth. As a loving deer and a grateful doe, let her breasts satisfy you all times, and always be enraptured with her love.

Being married is a lifelong learning experience shared with each other as you journey together. Just like anything new you start off by paying attention to details, putting the time and care into it that is needed. Then somewhere down the line it starts to become common and to you. Not that you necessarily take it for granted, but you get use to the idea of it being there. This is how we begin to see our marriage. We have been together so long or just that we have gotten familiar with the day to day that now it is a common place. You start going through the motions rather than continuing to put in the effort. Yes, marriage can be a type of investment, but like any investment it is not wise to go all in on it and then leave it to work itself out. Any investment needs to be tended to regularly to ensure that any issues you run across is dealt with quickly and timely. This is the same with marriage. Just because you know your spouse does not mean you should stop connecting with them. You start out praying together, laughing together, sharing your day with each other. Now you just walk past each other not as if you are disconnected, but as if you have gotten use to their presence. You assume they will be there regardless. We all have heard what you do to get them is what you must do to keep them. To an effect this is true. If you started out taking walks in the park, long uninterrupted conversations, opening doors, pulling out chairs, surprising each other with small, inexpensive gifts, foot rubs, back rubs, cooking, giving compliments, or even looking into each other's eyes to express your love; continue to do these things. You start strong trying to impress or sweep one another off your feet, but once you have spent a few years with this person the wooing stops.

I am a believer that what you continue to put work into will remain consistent. Yes, every now and again your marriage will need some maintenance to ensure your foundation is strong and secure, and it will require continued effort from the both of you. There is no such thing as a 50/50 marriage. Marriage is designed for both people to give one hundred percent. How do we do this when you feel there is not enough time in the day to give to one another? It is the little things, like to surprise your wife with a fragrance induced, sensual oil bubble bath. Not with the intentions of what you can get over, but with the intentions of her simply relaxing when she comes home. Intimacy does not start and end in the bedroom, but it starts when you wake up in the morning. You can get the flame started and keep it going all day until you see each other again. Who said that once you get married the flirting and dating stops? Send little love texts or emails during the day. Let them know they are on your mind.

We so easily get consumed with life and daily routines whether it be work or our children we burn ourselves out, leaving little to no energy left to share with each other. The ball has been dropped on the little things that kept a smile on our faces and the passion between the two dies out. That is what reading this book can help you with. No marriage can stand the test of time without prayer and a mind to work. The main ingredient is ensuring it remains strong and does not get weaker in prayer. You can pray separately as well as together. I am guilty of not praying with my wife as I should, but I know continued prayer is the preventative maintenance needed to have a long-lasting quality marriage. No one can ever say marriage will be easy, but one cliché you have heard that is wise to forget is "happy wife happy life". What life can be happy when happiness is only important for one person. We must get to a place where marriage is not about the venue of the ceremony, but it is about the destination the two of you desire to reach together as one. God created marriage as a covenant union that should be surrounded by love and his presence. I have learned this through the course of being married that lasting love starts when we concern ourselves with the well being of the other. You must have a genuine desire to see the two of you progress together without stagnation. We must remain with pure intentions in how we engage with each other in uplifting and interactions. A great marriage does not develop overnight but a marriage with a perfect love does blossom over time. Stand the course, remain vigilant watching for intruders trying to enter your marriage. When you feel that you have given your all remember that as vast as our minds are, we can never give everything we have. Continue to pull on God, continue to pull on each other. Love one another, cherish one another, and remember marriage is not a candle that melts away and it does not have an expiration date. The scripture tells us that when we have done all we can to stand, stand the more!

CHAPTER 12

How my Wounds Affected me

When you find yourself disappointed, betrayed, judged, and misunderstood that is a gate, an opening for hurt to take place in your life. In this chapter I will help you to see how your wounds will affect you in every area of your life. The gateway to hurt comes when trauma happens in your life. I have experienced several traumas throughout the course of my life. The first one was when I was born into a dissolved marriage. In my early teenage years (I was 14 years old) my father committed suicide and killed my aunt in the process of taking his own life.

My second trauma, all through my life I have heard "you are just like your father; you are out of control, bitter, and angry all the time." Not knowing who I really was (identity) and dealing with the hurt it began to affect me in ways one could never imagine. The lack of identity will have you thinking that you are not who God says you are, but you are what people say you are. I found myself constantly connecting with individuals due to the lack of discernment and identity. This would have me in relationships going in cycles year after year with dead end results. I would connect with friendships, (women and men) who were like minded in bashing other's, complaining, and not seeing the good in anyone.

The trust factor is an issue as well, I couldn't bring myself to trust those that I felt was a divine connection and was truly sent by God. These types of wounds kept me in a negative mindset about myself as well as others. I didn't seek and use discernment and common sense to make wise decisions.

In my work place I would not try my best in my work and would be angry. These wounds lead me to stagnation in my life. I wanted to go back to school, but because of my lack of commitment and the spirit of doubt once I finally went back to school, it took me over 20 years to finish and receive my master's degree. Procrastination is an issue that I find myself still dealing with, this came when I failed to get healing for my wounds.

Wounds will not allow you to walk into your full purpose in life. It will cause you to operate in fear and to be afraid of everything surrounding you. Fear has a way of crippling you, allowing you to make bad decisions, stay stagnant and miss all opportunities and possibilities.

2 Timothy 1:7

For God has not given us the spirit of fear, but of power and of love and of a sound mind.

Love is non-existent when you have wounds that you refuse to submit for healing. Don't allow your wounds to make you miss out on life. It will have you so twisted that you will start to doubt what God says about you. The scripture says, I created you in my own image (Genesis 1:27). You are fearfully and wonderfully made (Psalm 13: 14). I have had plenty of sleepless nights because of my wounds; given me nightmares of my past, especially experiencing the loss of my best friend and my 1st born son in the same year, that along with a divorce. I should be insane from all those wounds, but by the grace of God and my decision to seek healing for my soul, pushed me into a place of experiencing deliverance and healing.

We must address our wounds and move towards healing so that we can be free. In the next chapter, we will discuss healing pass the hurt and how you can start moving towards your healed place.

CHAPTER 13

Healing Pass Your Hurt

Once you make the conscious decision to move towards healing you will need to first confront the wounds that you have been experiencing. Lack of identity, trust issues, bitterness, fear, anger, and procrastination. Go back in your life and attach these characteristics to your hard places and your places of hurt. Once you identify them, don't stay there tormenting yourself in the memory of the wounds and hard places, but get the lesson of the hurt so you can give it to God and move forward.

One way to move pass your wounds to healing is to change your environment, you must change this both spiritually and naturally. If you know that the wounds are attached to a person, place or thing, then change that by forgiving the person for the hurt, forgiving yourself for the hurt. Make sure you surround yourself around those who are motivated, positive, and those who will push you forward away from your hurt.

Secondly, when establishing new relationships, friendships, and networks you must use the D word- Discernment. The definition of discernment according to Merriam Webster means the ability to judge well. You will need to make sure that you don't find yourself connecting with the same type of people, places or things that will create those past wounds.

No, you're not being paranoid or fearful, but you are simply maturing and being responsible for yourself. You will need to ask

God to show you the purpose of the person, place or thing and how it will be beneficial to your healed place and new life.

Thirdly, you need to CHANGE your mindset, and your response to negative and positive situations. In my pursuit of healing I had to change my mindset and believe what God said about me first. I had to change my mindset about the wounds in order to promote healing and not pull the scabs off the wounds when things didn't go my way or when adversity came. When going through the healing process the scab is there to help promote healing. There were many times that I would discern the person, but because I simply did not wait for God's voice or direction, I would re-injure myself therefore causing the scab to come off, which would have me back at square one. Healing is a process and you simply need to be patient with yourself, the process, and God.

During the healing process I found myself reading the word of God, meditating on it, praying, and seeking his face. During the healing process you want to ensure that you are staying consistent with the process and not deviating from it. If you need to see a License Professional Counselor (therapist) then by all means, see one. The therapist is held confidential, so it's safe to share your issues and wounds with your therapist. The therapist will assist you in learning building skills that will help you go through the process of healing.

I had the pleasure of speaking with a therapist that specialized in Trauma therapy when my 1st born was murdered in

2012. They helped me to look at his death in a way that I could grieve, but it also helped me to keep moving forward in life because I had other children that I needed to care for. She assisted me in talking about my son's death and push me to being open and honest about every feeling that I felt about such a great loss. The therapist pushed me into some mental breakthroughs which allowed me to put my wounds in perspective so that I could apply the healing process.

CHAPTER 14

My Healed Place

Healing is a process as we know however, there is a place called the healed place. In this place there is a newness of life for you. Being in your healed place allows you to be around those who have hurt you and you're able to talk about the experience without allowing the emotions to refuel the hurt.

In your healed place you should have peace and joy. You should be able to move forward in this place. There should be no stops, stagnation, procrastination, or negativity. In this place there should be healthy relationships and friendships. To be in your healed place you may have to break down your entire circle and evaluate all your associations with others. You should be able to make a wise decision to move forward in life (and not dwell on the past). In my healed place I spent a lot of time alone (not isolated) but focusing on me. Self-care was my focus in my healed place. I was wise with whom I allowed to have access to me, my time, money and possessions. I learned to say "No" and to discern the places that I frequented; especially if they served no purpose to my God given purpose. I made healthy decisions about my mind, body, and soul. This place should allow you to see the wounds, the healing, and give you the ability to be able to help others. Being able to help those that you are assigned to contributes to your testimony of healing. In this place you don't allow the healing to stop, continue walking in your healing and see it all the way through. Let affirmations go forth, songs of deliverance, praise, worship and prayer be your top priority in your daily devotion. Now that you are in your healed place continue to walk into your newness of life. Know how to deal with your wounds, position yourself, and protect yourself from future wounds.

CHAPTER 15

A Wise Woman Builds Her Marriage

If you desire a successful marriage you must learn to operate in the wisdom of God. In Proverbs 24:4 it tells us "By wisdom a house is built, and through understanding it is established; through knowledge its rooms are filled with rare and beautiful treasures." The word of God gives some specific plans for building a great relationship between husband and wife. It begins and ends with God's wisdom. Wisdom is the foundation on which a house must be built. It is the great principle on which all other principles must be founded.

Marriage is covenant institution designed by God, it is His heartbeat. He designed it. He established it and defined its boundaries. In marriage are two imperfect people joined together as one. There is no secret ingredient or magic potion that will make a marriage last. It takes wisdom, knowledge and understanding. The question lingers in the mind of many believers, what is wisdom? In Proverbs 9:10 it tells us "The fear if the Lord is the beginning of wisdom." I need the wisdom of God on how to build my marriage according to His blueprint. I need knowledge on how to structure and govern my marriage based on His word.

In Genesis when God caused a deep sleep to fall upon Adam, He took his rib and built woman, meaning God took his time and fashioned us into His likeness. God built woman to round out the man's incompleteness, so that physically, socially, emotionally, intellectually, and even spiritually, husband and wife would not be rivals, but mates. God has empowered us with such strength and endurance to be our husbands help meet for their success in life. As a wife we are built to cover our husbands' vital areas through prayer. We are created to complement each other.

As a wife we are the recipients of the deposits our husbands make in us. If there are no deposits, there can be no withdrawal! Therefore, with wisdom, knowledge, and understanding our ground must be cultivated to receive the seed that is sown. As a wife we must cultivate the fruit of the spirit in our marriage.

Galatians 5:22

"love, joy, peace, long-suffering, gentleness, goodness, faith, meekness, and temperance.

Proverbs 14:1

"A wise woman builds her house on seven pillars and a foolish woman tears it down with her hands."

The number seven represents completion and perfection, so we must always embrace the word of God with Wisdom, Knowledge and Understanding in order to build and construct our marriage on a solid foundation.

Pillar 1: Prudence- A wise woman who has sound judgement and self-restraint.

Pillar 2: Knowledge and Discretion- A wise woman who has keen perception, knows how to strategize, and formulate plans (meaning she knows how to plan for the future).

Pillar 3: Fear of God- A wise woman who reverence God by serving, worshipping obeying and loving Him.

Pillar 4: Counsel-A wise woman that gives good advice and guidance to others and one who also listens to wise counsel and instruction.

Pillar 5: Sound Wisdom- A wise woman lives upright before God, she has a proper understanding of things through observation. Her thoughts and conduct are both honest and pure.

Pillar 6: Understanding- A wise woman knows wisdom comes from the Father, she is a woman of intense and deep study, well educated in the word of God and she also has keen spiritual discernment.

Pillar 7: Power- A wise woman understands problems, but she has the ability to apply a God given solution.

As women we must become Wise Master Builders in our marriage and secure it with a strong and solid foundation which is the word of God.

Pray without ceasing!

CHAPTER 16

The Binding Together of Ish and Isha

(Man & Woman)

For the sake of time and space, let's begin with a very short synopsis of where we are headed and where we desire to end up for the benefit of all involved. We are addressing a divine order established at creation by God (Elohim) whose purpose was to benefit all of creation. Adam and Eve (Ish and Isha) were created by God (Elohim), before He spoke them forth. We understand this from Genesis 1:26-28. After God spoke concerning the purposes for which He was creating this order, we understand that Adam was formed from the dust of the ground. God blew into the male his breath of life and the male became a living soul. So, God (Elohim) breathes His soul into Adam and Adam became a "living" soul, a thinking, speaking body formed in the likeness (human stature), and image (intelligence) of God. Now let's begin to piece the puzzle together.

From Genesis Chapter 1:11-25, we see a powerful phenomenon taking place. God began to speak forth plants, trees and creatures, land, air and sea, commanding that each species created with seed must "produce after its kind". Here is where we want to jump into the basis of this writing. God created Adam and built Eve out of a rib which was taken from Adam. A charge was for these human specimens to reproduce "after their kind" and replenish the earth. Male and Female He created them. For the sake of clarity, we can safely say that the seed (sperm) was placed in Adam to "plant" in the ground (womb) of Eve and out of this power of creativity another speaking spirit (human being) would be re-produced (born). Every "seed bearing" plant, animal, bird, etc., would (reproduce) after its kind. A seed must be planted in the "proper ground" to produce a proper harvest. This is powerful, why? Because, as a man must plant his seed into the womb of a woman to produce a child (harvest), the same principle must be applied in every area of marriage.

Case in point. There is no place in the Word of God that states the wife must love her husband. The word speaks of the man loving the woman. The man must "plant" in the earth (mind) of the woman the desired harvest he wants to enjoy. Since every seed (words), will produce after its kind then that is how God designed man to receive all that he needs from his woman. However, he treats her and handles her or speaks to her that is the harvest he will receive. Woman was made with an emotional posture that can express itself in such a way that it would automatically pleasure her man. That's why she was taken from a vital place from within man. She covers his vital organs, his life sustaining organs, so that longevity would be his pleasure. If you look closely at the world you see that our electrical current flows from the same pattern. If a man (male counterpart), wants his lamp (lights) turned on he must plug his cord into the electrical socket and "Wala", the lights are on. It may sound funny, but it's a reality. Any electrical object needing an electrical current to operate must be "plugged" into an outlet where there's a current of power to produce what is needed to work (created power).

Husbands LOVE your wives, even as Christ loves the church and gave himself for it. Ephesians 2:25-28.

Husbands have the power to speak- not scream, shout or demand, but speak. Just speak the word (seed) into the womb (soul) of your woman and she's pre-programmed to give you a bountiful harvest.

CHAPTER 17

Purposed To Be Together

Matthew 19:6

"Wherefore they are no more twain, but one flesh. What therefore God hath joined together, let not man put asunder."

Her side: WARNING: DO NOT...I repeat DO NOT DATE YOUR FUTURE SPOUSE out of season. It does not take years to know if he or she is your future spouse. By then, the Lord has said yes, or no. Pay attention to the signs! After my husband and I got back together from our second breakup, it was definitely going to be our last. I had to sit still and allow God to take control. I knew for sure this was my husband. God had spoken to me in many ways. I was his rib. However, things looked like it was turning into another cycle until one day I looked him in the eyes and said, "Jamal, what are we doing? I'm here to become your wife." Months passed by and I was running out of patience. Right when I was about to call it quits, he finally confessed his reasoning for not asking for my hand in marriage--He didn't have enough money to afford my dream ring. When I heard those words, my heart dropped, and I was speechless. I, then, had to look myself in the mirror and say, "Kimberly, what is important... the ring or you become his help?" A lot of times we can focus on the material things and not the true meaning of the ring. So, I looked at my then boyfriend in the eyes, while swallowing my pride and told him, "If you buy me a three-hundred-dollar ring, I'll be the happiest girl alive." No, I wasn't settling; it was about me compromising and breaking the cycle of just "dating". So, we got that out of the way, and I was like, "Okay, wait... a month just passed! Are we still dating? Why?" While I was focusing on the way, all along my husband was still fighting! Lord! My patience was wearing thin. But then the devil began to make me feel as if I wasn't worthy of becoming a wife, and fear started to take over! I thought, well, maybe I'm not ready... what if he's gotten back to his old ways... Oh, my! What if we get a divorce?

But when I started to feel overwhelmed, I remembered God's promise. When I prayed before and covered those areas, He told me my prayers were granted. The Bible states, "And this is the confidence that we have toward Him, that if we ask anything according to His will he hears us. And if we know that He hears us in whatever we ask, we know that we have the requests that we have asked of Him" (1 John 5:14-15). If it's God, trust and believe everything will come to past that you desire!

Proverb 18:22

Whoso *findeth a wife findeth a good* thing, *and obtaineth favour of the LORD*.

His side: Fellas, I wasn't being honest. Again, it wasn't the money. I knew she was the one. God showed me multiple times! I couldn't imagine my life without her; she was perfect in my book. Yes, I know you're probably thinking: Well what is the problem? I'm Glad you asked! The problem was the very thing that stops people from reaching their very best... fear. When you allow fear to grip you, the enemy is having a field day in your mind! He will tell you all kinds of things just for you to turn and walk the opposite direction of your purpose! To even think of the responsibility of being a husband was terrifying. "Protector and provider" sounded easier said than done. The Bible states, "Anyone who does not provide for their relatives, and especially for their own household, has denied the faith and is worse than an unbeliever" (1 Timothy 5:8). I can't fail my wife! It's a must that I fulfill my role as a husband! This time I wouldn't be able to run!

Let's talk about the "run." Every time I messed up, I ran from the truth, because it was too hard being vulnerable! It hurts too bad to stare the truth in the eyes! When you look truth in the eyes you have to face your true identity! But as I prayed and asked for guidance, my faith grew, and fear began to cease from my mind. I declared and decreed that I would be a great husband, the best provider and a protector for my wife! I would not allow the enemy to step in!

Also, when I faced my true identity, I realized what my root issues were. I went through the healing process and I was able to get down on one knee! Don't be afraid to let go of the old you to be the best for your other half!

CHAPTER 18

Rebuilding from The Ground Up

As I enter into this new year, I cannot get over myself. I am floored, I am standing in the midst of my year end, reflecting. I always take the last two months of the year to reflect over where I started. This year we will be celebrating 5 years of Marriage and I do put emphasis on the word "we". I was always told the 5th year was the biggest milestone. See you don't know what I had to overcome; so, I am proud to say that we are standing here, but it is by the grace of God. We have made it to the 5-year mark! Every day I am truly amazed and honored how God has given my husband and I a second chance to appreciate the Gift of marriage. He said he would give me beauty for my Ashes (Isaiah 61:3) and he did just that. I know you have heard that everyone has a testimony? Well, I can attest to this. If you haven't read our story <u>Lovable Impressions: Hidden Dysfunction and Lasting Love</u> I suggest that you do so. You can read our personal testimony of what God has brought us out of. If you are silently struggling in your marriage and feel that your storm is about to take you out this is the book for you. In this book I share our marriage story- the up's, the downs, the struggles, the mishaps, and the short comings. I talk about how we went from a broken, hot mess to living each day creating Lasting Impressions. It is because of God's mighty touch and our obedience that we are here today, sitting in the midst of his glorious restoration. I know what it's like to struggle in marriage and be tossed to and from, but I also know what it is like to be fully restored.

From our story birthed my marriage ministry called: Lovable Impressions. It was birthed from my personal journey of marriage.

During that time, our word was Storm. So, we decided to take what our Father grew us through and share with others. At the start of every new year, I tend to ask my husband what is one word that he would use to describe the last season of our marriage. Our word for our marriage in 2017 was ship. To stay in the loop and get the latest updates and find out our word for the beginning of 2018 you can subscribe to the website: www.JasmineAddison.com.

Being that I have gone through so many transitions in the past two and a half years its only right that I share the "Now" with you all. Where are they now? We live in a world where marriage is put on a pedestal and idolized for all the glitz and glam the wedding day will bring that somehow, we tend to over-look the actual marriage and what it actually means to get married, to be married, and what it takes to stay married.

I tend to look at things through more than just my natural eyes so in these chapters you will read a lot of things that's beyond the natural. There's a bigger picture than what we see, the things that we are fighting are spiritual not practical.

My heart's desire is to see marriage be put back in right standing and have other marriages growing through the never-ending, forever evolving journey of love. Now the reason I say "growing through" is because I like to look at things on the Flip Side. My Natural eyes tell me that I am going through something, but if I Flip it to align with the word of God (Spiritual Eyes) then I know that every trial I endure is temporary and is needed for me to grow in the season that I am currently in which is then used to teach me something or prepare me for the next season of my life.

James 1:2-4
"Dear brothers and sisters, when troubles of any kind come your way, consider it an opportunity for great joy. For you know that when your faith is tested, your endurance has a chance to grow. So, let it grow, for when your endurance is fully developed, you will be perfect and complete, needing nothing."

Knowing how to survive the storm is one thing but preparing for a storm is a whole 'notha level. We always have some type of warning before any storm turns for the worst. For instance; the news outlets allow us to monitor the behaviors(signs) of any storm, this way we can get ahead and know how to properly prepare. It has been known for some storms to change overnight, but the warning signs were always there. If you do not properly prepare, then you will be stuck trying to survive. Let's just say this was the Addison's. We dived right into our marriage head first without the knowledge of what marriage was meant to be, how to weather the storms of life, or that there would ever be any storms to weather. However, when you decide to get married there are vows that both parties agree to and in those vows, we take is one crucial statement: (that we all tend to hear but not fully comprehend or process) For Better or For Worst. Now why didn't this statement stand out to us? It's not like we could have stopped to ask what's the extent of this part of the vow. Honestly, everyone's For Better or Worst is different. 99% of the time when you hear the word "Marriage" we don't tend to look beyond the wedding day. This is where most of everyone's focus is: The Big Day! Have you ever gotten to the place that you have spent so much time preparing for and you are in such awe? This was me, when I first boarded the ship, it was an exhilarating life changing experience. I was head over hills and just amazed by every aspect of it. However, just like spending time on any ship you tend to want to get off after you've been there for so long; you no longer want to rock and sway anymore, you don't want to hear the waves of water or the sounds of the winds blow, you just want to go back to dry land where you know it's comfortable at (at least I know I did). Well, after being on the ship, the experience quickly shifted. I found out that I wasn't about that life and we all know that being sea sick is no joke! In all honesty, the first two years we spent on the ship was the roughest due to not having a captain. We were so excited to board the ship that we did it with just us and all of our baggage.

We didn't know any of the ship's guidelines or policies and with all the baggage we boarded with we learned that it was just too much to fit onto the ship that it began to take on water. I didn't know the first thing about ships; not how to dock, steer, and I definitely didn't know how to ground it. I looked to my husband to have all of the answers, I mean who wouldn't. In my mind he was the protector so he should have been able to help us survive. Let's just say it was the blind leading the blind! Here we are both incapable of working together to properly save our ship. We took all the warning signs lightly, so we were unprepared. We both had things that we boarded this ship with that we valued too much to just throw any of the baggage overboard. Letting go of some of our baggage could have possibly salvaged our ship and stopped it from sinking. But of course, our sinking ship pushed us straight into survival mode. Now we all know what survival mode looks like right. It's where we don't properly know how to address a situation, and we're just to the point of trying to make it through. When life pushes you into situations that you are not prepared for or have no experience in you tend to panic under pressure. But isn't it the Captain's job to have an evacuation or rescue plan for his crew? Well, the problem with this was we were operating our ship without a captain and we were not licensed or trained to operate this ship, but yet here we were attempting to do so.

At this point I know you're thinking how did they board the ship without a captain? How did we even know how to disembark from the port? I'll tell you, we were so caught up in the awe of it all that we overlooked what it took to be on a ship. We failed to send an invitation to the Captain so that he could guide us and show us how the ship was meant to be navigated.

We were just two uneducated people trying to take what we both did not know and piece it together. Not knowing that we should have both gotten individual guidance from the captain so that we could have applied what we knew in order for the ship to sail smoothly. We decided the only way to survive and not go under with the ship was to jump ship. We barely made it to shore and now the coastguards are trying everything to selvage the ship, but the damage and debris was just too severe. We now had a choice, we could simply wait it out and try to repair what we already have, or we could just completely rebuild, starting from ground zero. This ship had been through the storm and back we couldn't just patch up the damages to it, it would cost us too much.

When you live in the same place for 25+ years, it's hard to see just how bad the damage is. But yet we tried, now he was awaiting the arrival of the inspector. The inspector came in and gave us the list of items (no questions asked) that must be replaced; the struggling of letting it all go was real. I mean we have operated with this equipment for several years, how can we possibly part ways with it? Once you have determined that you cannot reuse what you already have because it's too damaged, you must take your hands off and allow the restorer to come in and properly set things in order.

Rebuilding from the ground up isn't always easy and it requires many things from you: patience, dedication, and work. This isn't a job that can be rushed, it will take time. It won't be rebuilt overnight, so you must be dedicated enough to see the job through. If you are seriously wanting your ship to be rebuilt the right way you must be there ready to get your hands dirty, assist, and put in the work. Now it's time to rebuild our ship from scratch! The difference this time is that we both are aware and know that we are incapable of doing this ourselves. We need assistance.

The first thing we had to do was be honest during the inspection. There were things that we boarded this ship with that shouldn't have ever been a part of our journey (our baggage). Our baggage was over its weight capacity and had been packed into too many bags. Let's be honest, God cannot bless where you pretend to be. We had to allow the repairer the opportunity to come in and be able to do his job. This was the first step to building a solid foundation. Allowing God to become the captain of our ship was the best choice we had ever made since we've gotten married. Before you can start to rebuild, you have to first get out what's underneath the surface. The surface is where you house all of your baggage. This baggage needed to be thrown out and it was time to cut ties with the old things. This is a process and cutting corners to save time just won't do it. If you continue to take lessons from your captain, he will sustain you. Just remember not to get so caught up in receiving his resource that you don't allow yourself the opportunity to get revelation. These lessons will allow you to start building on solid ground.

So, rebuilding not only requires inviting God in the midst, it also requires you getting to work, throwing out the old things, and start to rebuild them with new. Now that you have begun the rebuilding phase you can start to build a Solid Foundation.

Self-Check:

Marriage is a sacred covenant between you, your spouse and God. Embrace everything marriage has to offer, it's a never-ending learning journey.

Thinking Point:

What are some areas of my life that I may be overlooking? Am I trying to be the Captain of my own ship? Have I allowed myself to be fully trained and guided by the Captain?

What changes can I make to ensure that God is the Captain of my Life and Marriage?

CHAPTER 19

Being Anchored on A Solid Foundation

Ecclesiastes 4:12 "Though one may be overpowered, two can defend themselves. A cord of three stands is not quickly broken."

Now that you are rebuilding its time to understand what it takes to build on a solid foundation and remain anchored. Many times, we are asked, "How did we do it?" How did we go from being shipwrecked to growing together in God? Often, we look for a complex formula for fixing our marriages when the answer is simple. I heard Steven Furtick say: "If you do what you knew." Many times, we have questions on how to save our marriage, but won't apply the things that we already know to do- Pray! During your time of trouble, it may sound like a cliché, but prayer is a powerful weapon. But before we get into the how let's talk about the what. Every ship has an anchor. The anchor's sole purpose is to prevent the ship from drifting due to the winds or currents.

It is vitally important that every marriage is anchored on a solid foundation. A foundation is known as being below ground level, the purpose of the foundation is to provide support and hold the structure together. The strength of your marriage lies within your foundation. In marriage, there will be times where you will be stretched far beyond your abilities, this is where your foundation comes in. No matter what kind of havoc blows your way your foundation must be strong enough that it will not collapse. I remember when I was younger, my Grandmother was preparing for a hurricane. Now this was the biggest hurricane that the town had seen in a very long time. I remember watching as the town prepared, one of the tasks they were all doing was putting duct tape on the windows. Now, as a child, I didn't know anything about how to prepare for a hurricane, so I didn't understand why duct taping the windows were so important. When I asked why I was told this is a technique that was a part of hurricane preparedness. Now this idea was set in place to prevent the windows from shattering into a million of pieces when the winds blew. Now this wasn't their foundation, but it was set to stop something that would have a major effect of shattering the glass into a million tiny pieces. It was later discovered that duct taping technique during a storm caused more harm than good. So, you see it is our job to safeguard our marriages just as we would safe guard our home during a storm. However, covering up the wounds with band-aids just won't suffice. Yes, it will stop the bleeding, but eventually the wound turns into a scab. It is not until the scab is pulled off that it can actually start its healing process.

Our anchor now became prayer. Growing together in God has given us both the ability to have discernment, handle issues differently, and even respond to one another differently during a storm of some kind. We are now able to see and hear clearly. Things that would normally bother us don't, we now have the strength to endure things that we never knew we had the ability to. We now know that we don't have to do it all ourselves. Laying your foundation is the most crucial stage when you start to rebuild. Starting over from scratch allowed us to see how we first used the wrong tools and equipment to lay our foundation. You have to take a look in the mirror and be willing to accept the ugly truth about the shortcuts you took.

Our ship has some costly parts that we can't afford to bargain with, and these parts must be replaced correctly. Now we began to think that it's not in the budget, but each part is needed to make the ship functional. Therefore, you have to be willing pay the price for what is needed to keep your marriage on the right track. There were a few parts that we learned were just not up for negotiating.

1. A Changed mindset

We hear every day that marriage is 50/50 and that is the only way that it can work. Marriage is a Compromise, etc. Marriage is not a business negotiation, you didn't sign a contract. You cannot negotiate and it is Not 50/50! Sorry, not sorry! We tend to take this thought because simple math tells us that 50 + 50 gives us 100. You should never go into your marriage thinking that you should only give 50% of you and that your spouse should meet you half way with the other part of it. Marriage is 100/100. Each spouse should always give the other the best of themselves. We both had to committed to giving our marriage 100%.

2. Cover your Marriage

Now you are in a place where you should have invited the captain onto your ship, but are you communicating with him (Prayer)? Cover your spouse through prayer, it is your weapon.

Prayer is essential. We must have a fixed focus on the captain of our ship. Allow him to do his job and be our guide. Be one another's covering it will help you through tough times.

3. **Godly Council**

Be mindful of who you surround your marriage with. Surround your marriage with those who support it. You didn't put in all the work of laying down a solid foundation just to have those around you tear it up. Your friends and family should be supportive and know that in any marriage you will have disagreements. They must also know what it means to be married, how scared a marriage is, and the importance of the vows that you took. Your friends and family should also give you sound advice, not feed your flesh.

4. **Die to your Flesh Daily**

Read: Colossians 3: 1-19

Our old self isn't nearly as good as our new self. Putting on our new self and walking in Christ allowed us to get rid of the poor behaviors which were preventing us from having a healthy marriage. We live in a fallen world, so we want to ensure that we aren't responding through our flesh.

Marriage is a lifelong, evolving journey. No matter what obstacles your marriage face know that you can face them together. Marriage is work, but when 100% from both husband and wife are given the reward in the end is everlasting.

Having to rebuild our marriage from the ground up has helped us learn many valuable lessons, one being appreciating our marriage much more. My marriage is something I will never stop pouring into. Through our experiences we were able to learn and grow. We are now equipped with the tools we need to fight. This helps us to ensure that our marriage is a kingdom marriage and yours can be too.

Thinking Point:

What is anchoring your marriage?

What are you building your Foundation on?

What changes do you need to make to ensure you have a solid foundation?

Self-Check:

How much am I pouring into my marriage? Am I safeguarding my marriage?

Lord,

I thank you for giving me the ability to share my journey with others. I pray that my testimony helps them to continue to build a lasting love, that they know this fight is a spiritual one and not physical one. That they are using the tools to build and rebuild their marriages daily including you as the captain of their lives and union.

CHAPTER 20

The Jagged Emotions of a Man

> *"Be devoted to one another in love. Honor one another above yourselves." – Romans 2:10*

Growing up as a child we are taught at a young age to be strong; to show no emotion, because emotions are a sign of weakness. As men we are told and expected to not show love because "love will get you killed." Society has perverted us into thinking that men should not have any type of emotions. So, we began perverting our identities and portraying that we don't have any emotions for the sake of others. This allows us to portray that we aren't seen as being weak. The reputation of a man is built upon them being strong and masculine, them being able to carry the weight of the world on their shoulders. This makes us feel the need to detach and withdraw ourselves emotionally. Being detached from your emotions is dangerous. You tend to hold everything in and teach yourself how to detach from emotionally connecting with others. By choosing to do this we are perverting ourselves from being able to love, let alone expressing our love for others. How can one with no emotions freely give or receive love? How can one who cannot show love, or have emotions love themselves? Being that I couldn't show any emotions or love it was hard for me to love myself because that meant I would have to be attached to some sort of emotion.

> ***"My command is this: Love each other in the same way I have loved you." - John 15:12***

Growing in Christ has taught me many things about myself. Being able to fulfill this commandment meant that I needed to first rid myself of the ways of the world. I had to learn how to break the cycles that I was accustomed to. In order to do this, I had to allow my Father who is love the ability to show me how to love and how to accept being loved. I spent twenty-eight years living my life being emotionally detached. Being able to reflect over my life revealed to me how this was preventing me from truly being able to love, trust, or even communicate with my wife. I carried around hidden emotions and I was unable to love my wife on the level that she needed to be loved. Surrendering to my Father allowed him to heal me and make me whole which in return opened up the tunnel of love.

I was now able to love freely and allow myself to feel emotions. I was able to open up emotionally and learn to express those emotions to my wife. Being able to express myself was new. The problem with this was being that I was never loved or had any emotions that once I learned that it was ok to show the emotions; I soon became overwhelmed with them. I could express myself, but the passion behind expressing myself was the challenging part. Being able to shut my emotions off was easy I mastered this ability, but being able to compartmentalize them was hard. I didn't know how to handle my new-found emotions. As a man who doesn't know how to express himself; I was stuck. There were many times when I tried to control my emotions and it hindered me. My love quickly turned to passion. I found myself being rather passionate about a lot of things which caused me to express myself harshly rather than intimately.

Love can take many different shapes and forms. My love was all over the place, it was jagged. I called this form of emotion jagged edges. Jagged edges are sharp, uneven, and misplaced. Jagged edges can be anger, miscommunication, lack of communication, hitting below the belt, and unspoken expectations. My emotions were misplaced, causing my love to be sharp. Not knowing how to express myself made me say things that came out harshly. I meant well but the words didn't come out that way.

The ultimate goal is to be able to express ourselves in ways that leave impressionable marks on our spouse heart that would last for a lifetime. It's meant to be a beautiful, growing journey, but you must first know how to express your emotions correctly. I now had the emotions, but I wasn't connecting these emotions intimately with my wife. Intimate emotions allow us to connect with our spouse on an emotional level. Being emotionally intimate with our spouse makes room for the threads of our life to become intertwined with one another which then allows us to begin to express ourselves deeply.

> *"So, they are no longer two, but one flesh. Therefore, what God has joined together, let no one separate." -Matthew 19:6*

This love was new but yet an exhilarating, magical expression of love. Leaving impressionable marks on our spouse's heart when not properly channeled can be in a form of love or it can also be in a form of pain and hurt which can leave scars. Building strong emotional bonds in our marriages are the building blocks to creating lasting love.

Strengthening my emotional intimacy in my marriage became my ultimate goal. Having a strong, emotional, intimate bond in my marriage was needed for both my wife and I. It allowed me to be ok with being vulnerable, but it also strengthened me as a man, husband, and a father. This was the start of building a strong, happy, and healthy marriage. Men are allowed to have emotions. We are allowed to Love and more importantly, we are allowed to be intimate with our love. Yes, even with emotions and love we are still strong. Love starts when you find refuge in God which then allows us to tunnel it into our home. It is our job to express and show it in a manner that teaches our children that they are our next generation and we should be planting the seeds of love in their lives.

Thank you so much for taking out the time to read this book our prayer is that the testimonies that were shared, and words of wisdom was a blessing to you. If you would like more information on any of the authors or the mission of Lasting Love, please email Morgan Jefferson at mjmanagement81@gmail.com.

www.ingramcontent.com/pod-product-compliance
Lightning Source LLC
LaVergne TN
LVHW051507070426
835507LV00022B/2976